STORIES OF THERE AND THEN

Tales and memories
from a 2013 intergenerational writing course

Edited by Cathy Fowley

WOODENHOUSE
Publishing

Published by Wooden House Publishing Ltd
Dublin, Ireland, contact@woodenhousepublishing.com

Stories of There and Then
Tales and memories from a 2013 intergenerational writing course
Edited by Cathy Fowley

Typeset by Wooden House Publishing Ltd
Cover illustration and design by Raphaël Savina

ISBN13: 978-1-910564-00-4 (Paperback - Print on demand)
Print on demand technology is a high-quality, innovative and ecological printing method; with which the book is never 'out of stock' or 'out of print'.

ISBN13: 978-1-910564-01-1 (Ebook)

British Library Cataloguing-in-Publication Data.
A cataloguing record for this book is available from the British Library.

To our families, then and now

CONTENTS

CONTENTS

CATHY FOWLEY

EVERYONE HAS A STORY TO TELL

In October 2012, a group of students started a new writing module in Dublin City University. Nothing unusual at first glance. Yet, in an environment where mature students are those over 23, this class gathered learners in their 60s, 70s and 80s as part of the Intergenerational Learning Programme. The ILP had started 4 years earlier as a pilot project, with the aim of opening the university to people over 55 who may never have had the opportunity to attend college earlier in their lives. Various modules were on offer, and plenty more would be added in years to come. The programme was designed as a way to open new knowledge to seniors, but also as the means of valuing and transmitting their experience to a younger generation. Arising from a wealth of lived experience, professional, technical or life skills were shared between generations. Older participants' experience, however, also opened a window into the past, as they shared memories from their youth, a time that a lot of younger people now see as history. They are the witnesses of a social history which too often remains untold.

Everyone has a story to tell. Many of the people we meet in our daily lives are true storytellers; they can recount the mundane and the everyday with flair and gusto, and they can make a bus trip into town sound like an adventure. Some have lived extraordinary lives, far removed from our experience. In other cases, life stories sound fascinating because of the time they were lived in; suddenly, through a memory, a snapshot of a moment, places which are familiar, take on a different shape. The streets of Dublin echo with cattle sounds on their way to the ships; in the kitchen, food is kept in a pantry, and grandparents are children at the gate, looking at their own grandparents, a vista of time offered to us. Whether we know them, or we read about strangers' lives, other people's stories are echoes of the human condition.

The story of our life is one we tell constantly, it becomes who we are. Everybody has a story to tell, and everybody is a story. We all love to hear them, and feel we should read them too: "there's a book in there, you should write that down". Every grandmother and grandfather is also the keeper of family stories. As families scatter and children leave home, the myths and stories that bind the family slowly disappear. "You should write that down".

The authors of the stories in this collection did just that. These stories belong to a shared place, and a shared past. They wrote them down as part of a group; they wrote for each other, for themselves, for their families, and to keep the stories alive while telling of universal life experiences. These are stories of innocence and stories of loss, stories of love and families, stories of hopes and disappointments, stories of courage in the face of adversity, stories about the beauty and intrinsic value of the everyday, of the buttermilk, the train journey. These stories of past times engage us to take the time to experience and value our own lives. And to learn how to tell our stories.

DAN REDMOND

....

OUR MOTHER

Our father had found employment with Harry Ussher, known to his staff as the "Big Fella", owner of an estate which incorporated a racing stable. Our father's wage was two pounds per week, tenancy of a tied house and a condition that our mother would milk eight cows morning and evening six days per week.

Our mother, having attended Ramsgrange boarding school in County Wexford in which she had excelled in animal husbandry, was a marvel as a cook, a seamstress, a knitter, a baker, and a jam maker. She was a competent aid at a birthing, and the laying out of the departed. She played camogie for Wexford in 1922-23. She smoked 20 Woodbines a day and would wager her shirt on two flies climbing up a wall. I believe that same College with its pupils largely from the farming communities –with most of the wealthy farmers owning a couple of hunters and chasers– were responsible for her gambling, a weakness she brought with her to the grave.

Of course a racing stable was the last place she should have been, because every time a saddle was thrown on one of Ussher's horses the enthusiast stable lad would always give the nod no matter if the horse was minus a leg.

Her family had been well off until the twenties with a good farm and a business, their clients being the establishment, the business evaporating in the tumult of the age. The farm, through our grandfather's fondness of liquor, was sold in lots until reduced to 30 acres. She blamed her personal misfortune on the day she saw a rough-looking bowsey with his cap at a rakish angle giving her the eye. Yes; our father.

She had a complex character and was subject to random bursts of rage –annulled by a constant self-sacrifice and acts of warm-hearted benevolence. She was intelligent, compassionate and had common decency by the bucket-full. She was also stubborn and naïve –all of which could be verified within an hour when under pressure, which seemed to be most of the time.

She was also afflicted with the Mr Micawber syndrome, of keeping herself buoyant with the surety that something wonderful (including money) was going to turn up. I clearly recall one morning as she dressed the beds, her looking out and seeing that the postman had passed without stopping, and she remarked in anger "Blast him anyway; there goes the shagger without leaving a letter" as if he had a bag full of letters for her but for some reason would not deliver them.

Her childish pleasure and naivety was witnessed at a ritual every Monday afternoon when Charlie Smithers, Joe Farrell, Terry Hayes and Jackie and Billy Tyrell, plus others, would gather around our fire after exercising their horses, although it was too early to feed them and was also before our mother's milking time. Charlie would relate the film he had seen in Bobby McDonald's –a wood-built cinema in Swords with the principal man being the "Chap" and the heroine the "Mott". Charlie, in his flat unemotional voice would paint the most wonderful adventures and acts of heroism, of romance and heart-break, filling our imagination with astonishing scenarios. Indeed, one particular film, titled "Rosanna of the seven moons" had our mother repeating the same for ages afterwards whenever she'd get someone to listen. Charlie, from Whitehall and aged about 18 at the time –a taciturn, serious, and utterly decent young fellow– was a brilliant purveyor of the art, and art it was.

Our mother, quite by accident or perhaps by her impulsive disposition, talked herself into further slavery. It arose when an owner came to view his horse which it seems wasn't living up to his expectations. He was also displeased with the ragged, neglected state of the beast's blanket –apparently reflecting the horse's position in the stable regime– a backyard no hoper. Jack, the head lad, was embarrassed, as was Johnny Dooley, the manager. Indeed, the "Big Fella" himself as well, for although these particular clients were not too important, their fees for stabling were. The stable maintenance routine saw that from time to time their blankets were sent somewhere to be upgraded, a prolonged and expensive exercise.

Our mother on hearing about the furore, and to help "poor Jack", suggested to him she might be able to do something with them, and she did. Although she could do nothing with their shabbiness she otherwise left them as new. I remember these events vividly as one incident concerning the blankets relates to the first time I saw the sea.

It came about that the stable had four runners at Baldoyle and, discovering the horse blankets were in shreds, Johnny Dooley pleaded with our mother to do instant repairs. This request was the day before racing. Most of her night was spent repairing two; the fabric with its leather trimming, very difficult to stitch, had to be done by hand. The other two, partially repaired, she promised would be ready before the horses were paraded. At ten the next morning three of us set off walking through the woods of the estate and out through the Naul road exit, pushing a pram with wrapped bread and butter sandwiches, Frank (an infant) and the two blankets. Our journey took us through Forest Great, Cloghran, and on to Kinsealy, where we met the agitated travelling lad Paddy Oakes, who grabbed the blankets and shot away in the "Big Fella's" shooting brake.

Our mother then decided, for a treat, we'd visit the seaside for our picnic and about an hour later we found ourselves in Malahide. God! I couldn't get over the immensity of the sea –how sound carried, the smell of the seaweed, the odd yacht far off. At that time the seashells were so large and numerous they were a hazard for barefoot walkers. I also well remember the five mile walk home, most of the way with two of us in the pram.

Johnny Dooley was always well turned out as his position required. A daily white shirt and its detachable collar were imperative to his status. But the efforts of the Blue Swan laundry included tearing your collars to pieces in no time and returning your shirts button-less.

Yes, our mother began to look after his shirts and collars. Then Joe Hogan's —Joe being a steeple-chase jockey. Then she was inveigled to do the lads', about a dozen of them. She was then asked by Johnny to upgrade his Harris Tweed jacket with leather elbows —including cuffs with leather trimming. Appeals were made for the turning of shirt collars and overcoats. Lengthening or shortening of trousers and britches became the order of the day. Mostly for nothing. The unfortunate lads had nothing to give but by way of reward would saw a heap of logs for our fire or go to the well for her whenever she asked. Johnny and Joe would be generous by slipping the odd ten bob note into her hand. She was a Trojan to work, and intensely concerned with the quality of it.

One afternoon Joe Hogan came into our kitchen wearing a new wool polo-necked jumper, standard in the racing world. Where's the old one Joe? Our mother asks. "It's in my room ready to be dumped" Joe replies adding a 'why' at the end. "I'll get a pullover for one of the kids out of it" she says; and she did. Indeed there's a photo somewhere of our younger brother Billy wearing a recycled pullover for his holy communion. The unravelling of these garments was always a pain. As our mother unravelled, one of us had to rewind the wool into balls, a tedious, boring exercise.

I clearly recall her, week in week out in our backyard with a washing board in the galvanised bath, it rocking on a backless chair, she with a bar of Sunlight soap happily scrubbing and singing until her nail-less fingers were raw. Her labour resulting in about fifteen shirts hanging on the line, and if a cloud appeared she'd blast it out of the sky. Later the laundry would be taken inside to be pressed with a couple of solid irons. All that labour for the sum of six shillings which Johnny had negotiated, with half the money ending up in Bobby Savage's, the bookies in Swords.

She was a capable woman, doing so much for the challenge and the joy of it. She would justify her efforts by announcing it was a way of paying homage to Jesus for the gift of life. I believe the preoccupation kept her anxieties at bay, a subconscious method of dealing with pressure. Her own mother was of a similar character, renowned for her common decency, hard work, and generosity of spirit. While our mother was religious and very conscious of her every act and word being monitored by Jesus, she was not a zealot. In our school days during the season of Lent she would dragoon us into saying the rosary every evening after tea —all five decades. God! It was so boring and uncomfortable, kneeling on that flagged floor of our kitchen, and no way of avoiding it. She was always involved in this novena or that one, still among her belongings the hand-written prayers. To sum up, I firmly believe she possessed a subliminal spirituality inculcated by generations into doing the decent and generous thing.

NUALA SMITH

TO BE FRANK

In this one you are sitting on a photographer's couch, posed in what is a very formal pose for a boy of four. Your eyes are huge and dark, your expression anxious and somehow, cowed. It's as if you'd been warned to behave, or else.

You're a good-looking child, your hair thick and curly, you face has the makings of the handsome man you will become. Your small boy legs, which are posed, sideways, with one knee bent, look gangly in your short pants.

On the back of this picture, given to me by your younger brother's wife, there's a date stamp; Drogheda 1922.

We stare at it, your granddaughter and I, and wonder how such a small boy could ever have become the man I knew as 'Da'. My daughter, born too late, could only hear the stories about you. And there are many of them.

Francis Smith, or Frank as he was known, was the architect of the life we, his family, lived, the effects of which echo to this day. The shadow of the disgrace of such a father, fell over all three of us, in various ways.

Our mother, carefree and fun-loving when she married Frank at twenty-one, was catapulted from the stern security of a city home and successful business, to a tumult of insecurity in the village of Bettystown, near Drogheda.

As children, we girls longed to hear the romantic details of how our parents met. But our mother was always dismissive, putting everything down to "the War".

As they'd married as World War 2 was raging, we had to be content with this closed book. No extravagance could have been countenanced during the horrors of a war. We accepted this, feeling deep pity for her, cheated out of her 'big day' by the monster, Hitler.

Not long after our mother died at seventy five, my sister investigated what she'd long suspected. Our parents' marriage certificate showed their first-born arriving seven months after their wedding. There's no one to ask now anyhow. But that simple date put another shadow over the never-talked-about wedding in 1942.

So how did you meet her? I ask the little boy in the photo. How did you find and marry that carefree girl, Carmel Fagan from 15 Ushers Island on the quays in Dublin?

You were twenty-four then. Very tall, thick black hair, oiled in the style of the day. Hazel eyed, slightly round-shouldered, showing the shyness that dogged you. But handsome, and well-off, from a large farm in Louth, and you, the eldest son.

To us, our mother's story was that Frank was sent with truck loads of grain to her father's business, old Peter Fagan being a corn merchant on Dublin's Quays.

I imagine you now high up in the cab of the lorry, grinning down at the petite Carmel who was always 'hanging around the yard'. The youngest of four sisters and a brother, she was a bit forgotten about and used to amuse herself, wandering into the barn or the stables, with her mongrel 'Tatters'.

Her father was a typical Victorian. Strict and deeply religious, he built up a successful business from nothing, before the Rising of 1916.

Nationalism was of no interest to him, most of his corn being sold to the resident British army. But as Ireland was about to win its independence, he made the most of his opportunities, his success providing total, if discreet, security for his family.

In any of our mother's accounts of her home life, I never heard her mention any form of love. Family life was stern and orderly and 'Da' ruled his kingdom with an iron rod. His children were all terrified of him.

In my album there are photos of Peter Fagan too, in which he appears bowler-hatted, rotund, with protruding eyes, and does indeed look completely unapproachable.

So, could stern Peter Fagan be part of the reason my mother fell for you? Apart from the fact that you were handsome, you were also shy. But as to your first date, your courting, or even the extraordinary probability that Carmel was pregnant before she married you, all this is shrouded in mystery now.

There are no wedding photographs, no mention of where they spent their honeymoon —or even if they had one. All I know is that Frank took his bride to live in a thatched cottage in Bettystown. Again 'the War' was blamed. The cottage in Bettystown was all that was available. Damp and unelectrified as it was, it was to be only temporary.

So how long was it before things began to go wrong? How long did bliss last? Was there any bliss?

Settled in Bettystown and pregnant, Carmel must have felt as though she'd been exiled from the world. Her three unmarried sisters were still at home in Dublin. She knew no one in this country town. Her husband was away every day, working on the family farm outside Drogheda. But as time went on, she began to realise that he was not sick when he came in glazed and unsteady. He had been drinking; was in a state unfamiliar to her, drunk or in various stages of being drunk.

And so began her impossible battle, trying to reform an alcoholic who does not want to be reformed. Her children were born, first a girl, Brenda, who inherited her father's good looks, then a boy, Breffni, who died a cot death at six months, then a second daughter, myself, Fionnuala. All this within the space of four chaotic years, during which time our mother somehow managed to stay afloat while Frank continued on his reckless course of destruction.

While Carmel was in the local hospital having me –her third– Frank was in the men's ward with a broken leg sustained as he'd cycled into a ditch on his way home. How this happened was a dreadful source of embarrassment to her.

Visiting her sisters in Dublin by train soon after, her babies in tow, she returned to find that her house had been burgled. Long afterward the mysterious robbery was explained to her by her neighbour –the culprit named was Frank.

So the downward spiral went on, until, after a terrifying episode when Frank took aim at Carmel with his shotgun, her sisters reluctantly offered her refuge in their large home in Dublin. The condition was that Frank was not included. And so we moved in with them, leaving him to struggle in his new job as a travelling salesman, living, when not on the road, in a bed and breakfast in Drumcondra –his work on the family farm having mysteriously dried up.

Here my memories of you are clearer. On how many Saturdays did you drive up in your black baby-Austin and park outside the aunts' house? Mother and we small girls walk out the back gate to you and the Saturday drive to the Phoenix Park begins. Club Orange on the way home and then back into the kitchen to share the rest of the evening with aunts Peggy and Celia's rules, as you drive away.

We took it as normal until the day a child in my class at school pointed to you in the photo of our aunt's wedding I'd brought in to show the nun.

"That man lives in our house" little Marion O'Neill announced to the gathered children and I was inexplicably mortified.

I became aware of what drunk meant one horrible evening when you arrived but then we didn't go for our drive. We girls were sent upstairs where my sister pulled me into our bedroom, slammed the door and said, in a very cross voice,

"Daddy's drunk!"

All these years later, I still remember feeling completely mystified, but sure that this must be my fault.

Eventually our mother did manage to leave her sisters' grudging shelter and find a house –the solution, you said, to your drinking. If you had a home with us, you would settle down and stop drinking forever. You even went with Carmel to two AA meetings.

But within six months of our moving in, you were as bad, if not worse than ever. Sacked from the job, every neighbor you could touch for a loan, contacted, and the endless round of staggering in on the few evenings you made it home. And our mother pregnant again.

So she put you out. After nearly twelve years, Carmel finally accepted that this was the only way. Giving an alcoholic chances, she'd discovered, was a pointless exercise. Brave woman that she was, pregnant with virtually no financial support, she 'encouraged' you to 'try Manchester'.

I remember the night you left us. It is November, we three sit around the fire in the back room. You are lingering in the doorway, your case held, still hoping for another reprieve. My swollen mother and my sister, now thirteen, sit staring into the busy flames. Torn as ever, I ask to go to the bus stop with you. The two heads at the fireside don't look round. Feeling like a traitor, I go with you anyway. It's foggy, the street lights are orange, turning yellow.

"Me oul pal" you call me, looking down and squeezing up your eyes in a smile that might be you starting to cry. When you step on the bus I cry as I turn to run back home, yet I'm glad you're gone too.

And then silence. Then some presents, silly ones according to mother, who, to our horror sends back a manicure set, and two lipsticks.

Then you are spotted, on one of your two visits back, in our front garden with your head in your new son's pram. We run to lock you out. You plead through the door. But it's no good.

In my twenties, I find you in Manchester. In the bar where we meet you are drinking quietly, cigarette smouldering between yellowed fingers. "The shadah in the corner" you call yourself with a spluttered cough and that grin.

KIERAN DUNNE

CLICHES

When all is said and done, the bottom line is, that at this point in time, at the end of the day, there is light at the end of the tunnel. The elephant in the room, however, raises the roof. This sets the cat among the pigeons. The pigeons are feathering their own nests. One pigeon, however, out on a limb, falls and upsets the apple-cart which is pulled by a horse of a different colour. The dog starts barking up the wrong tree, and the other dogs in the street know that something is wrong. Then the winds of change come, creating a storm in a teacup. Not for all the tea in China could the farmer face the music, so he flies off the handle.

When the chickens come home to roost, the farmer's wife spills the beans. Her goose is cooked as she puts things on the long finger. However, the angry farmer bites off more than he can chew. She strikes while the iron is hot and, despite a soft landing, the farmer is no longer viable.

KAY PHILPOTT

CHILDHOOD HOLIDAYS

ONCE UPON A TIME there was a little girl who was afraid of trains. Big noisy trains with loud shrieking whistles, belching out clouds of damp smoke. The little girl lived in the centre of the City, but once every summer she travelled down to Wexford for her holidays with her father, mother and younger sister.

She really looked forward to her holidays but she knew that in order to get there, she had to endure the ordeal of meeting THE TRAIN.

It was wartime and, even if her parents had been wealthy enough to own a car, they couldn't use it, because petrol was rationed, only being doled out to those who really needed it for work purposes. And long-distance buses were few and far between. So, the train it had to be, even though it, too, travelled precariously on turf fires, often wet and unreliable, with many delays and unscheduled stops.

Her mother would start admonishing her as they walked to Harcourt St. Station, she holding the little girls by the hand, while Daddy wheeled his bicycle alongside them with their suitcases piled high on top of it.

"No need to start crying now –there's nothing to be afraid of. It's just the noise of the wheels on the track. Don't upset your little sister!"

But as they climbed the steps up to the station, the little girl was filled with a mixture of trepidation and anticipation. Dad bumped his bike up the steps, parking it by a wall to be watched over by Mammy and the girls, while he went to get the tickets. Then they went on to the station platform, until the huge monster pushed its way in, heaving and wheezing and belching out steam, while the little girl clung to her father's trouser-leg, cowering and whimpering in terror. At last the squealing would stop, the dreadful noise replaced by the shouting and banging doors. Daddy would then put his bike in the guard's van while they climbed into the small carriage of eight seats (no corridors in those trains!) and the little girls settled down to read the Mickey Mouse comics he had brought back with him.

Then the journey would start and they'd be off with the piercing whistle fading in the distance, and only the comforting puff-puff sound accompanying them on their way.

I was that little girl and we were going to spend our annual fortnight's holiday with my great-aunt Jane, my Dad's aunt, in Inch, near Gorey.

As we travelled along I marvelled at the advertisements for Virol and Players Gold Flake cigarettes on the stations, but never the name of the station itself. This was wartime after all and we must fool the enemy by not letting him know his location. I never could figure out how Dad knew when we arrived at Inch station, but once we left the train, laden with cases and the bicycle, there was Aunt Jane with her donkey and cart, ready to convey us the three miles to her house.

To reach the house from the gate we had to negotiate our way, through the farmyard, past various hens, geese and sometimes turkeys wandering around, a somewhat frightening experience for us city children, but one which we got used to during the following days. The house was single storey and our bedroom opened off the living-room. There was no electricity, just oil lamps and at night the door was left open a comforting crack, so we were able to hear the adults as they sat around the open fire, chatting and occasionally telling hair-raising ghost stories about the area, which Aunt Jane swore were true. These almost always involved a story about a headless horseman who could be seen, but not heard as he wandered the roads at night, and they made us shiver as we listened to the strange silence of the countryside, broken only occasionally by the soughing of the wind in the trees out in the eerie darkness. Indeed, on one occasion, before the outbreak of war, my uncle had proudly acquired a car in which he drove down to bring us home. On the way back, through Wicklow, late at night, we got a puncture. He and Daddy got out to mend it in the pitch blackness and meantime a horseman rode past, the horse's hooves making no sound on the grass verge. As we couldn't see the man's head from our position in the car, we thought, for many years afterwards, that we had seen The Headless Horseman!

Aunt Jane had been a cook in a "Big House" before her marriage and we marvelled at her wonderful cooking on the open fire. I can still taste the lovely jams, soda bread and porridge she produced from pots balanced on a trivet over the flames. We didn't need much encouragement when she asked us to turn the bellows to keep the fire going!

Every afternoon, as soon as milking time was over, my sister and I would be dispatched to Mrs. Boland's farmhouse for the milk. This was about half a mile away and we'd argue over which of us would carry the milk can. As soon as Mrs Boland invited us in she'd ask us which Irish dance we learned in our class since she saw us last. Down she'd take her fiddle from its spot on the mantelpiece as she launched into a reel or jig encouraging us to display our prowess, after which we'd be rewarded with cup of fresh milk, as she and her grown-up daughters applauded our efforts. Then we'd set off back to Aunt Jane's as twilight descended under the overhanging trees and we did our best to hurry past the remains of a dead rat we once spotted at the side of the road, which grew flatter and flatter but didn't entirely disappear, as the days passed. Indeed much milk was slopped from the sides of the can as we ran past.

Another thing that amazed us was the lack of shops, so it was very exciting for us to see the mobile shop enter the yard once a week.

We watched Aunt Jane haggling with Mr Gregory over her groceries. Anything she didn't get from him was bought on Sunday morning after Mass in Lee's shop beside the Church in Castletown. Castletown was about three miles further on from our base in Clonough and once again the donkey was tethered to the cart to convey us to Mass on Sundays. Occasionally we elected to walk, but sooner or later, some kind neighbour would offer us a lift in a pony and trap. Inside the little church the men would kneel on one side and the women on the other, and if the priest was long-winded, the men went outside for a smoke during the sermon.

And so our holiday went on, accompanying our parents to friends' houses for tea in their best parlours, and walking a few miles to the seaside sometimes with some of the local children. These were usually the Kavanagh girls, whose farm we passed on our way. As we walked down the lane towards the strand, the grassy stones beneath our feet would gradually turn sandy until we crossed the dunes, and there, glistening before us, was the sea. We couldn't wait to get into the water and would tuck our skirts into our knickers as we ran into the waves. Of course, in the manner of all childhood memories, the sun was always shining then. When we had enough of the water, Mum would produce sandwiches and milk fresh from the cow, a picnic which was always welcome.

All too soon the two weeks would pass. We now considered ourselves proper country children, collecting the hens' eggs every morning and even knowing where to look when they were "laying away" from the nests. And we even knew how to call the donkey in from the field. So that was our sad chore on the day we were returning home, to get Jenny-Jo ready to bring us back to Inch station and the trip back to Dublin on the dreaded TRAIN.

VERA HICKEY

THE HOUSE
WITH THE GOOD BUTTERMILK

When I close my eyes I can still see the old rambling farmhouse vividly, with its corridors, its nooks and crannies, and so many small rooms upstairs. Outside there was a huge barn with a ladder up to the loft. I have many happy memories of the Kelly family who lived there with their ten children, four girls and six boys.

Jean and I used to go there often. We were best pals, and our houses were next door to each other. Our mothers were also close friends. Both of them did a lot of baking, and always needed buttermilk. Someone told them of the great buttermilk you could get at Kelly's farm, so Jean and I were sent off to get some with our two milk pails with lids. The farm was about two miles away, so it was a long road. However, we discovered very quickly that we could get there through the fields in half the time. We used to go about twice a week for the buttermilk. We were always brought into the farmhouse, and over the weeks the visits became less about buttermilk, and more about just loving to be there.

We became very friendly with the girls, particularly with Rita who was about thirteen, the same age as ourselves. We helped them to collect eggs, and feed hens, and go out to the fields to bring their brothers tea and sandwiches. I think that was the first time I felt the thrill of being with boys.

The boys used to throw hay at us, or run at us, and try to catch us, and we were always careful not to run too fast. Jean and I loved it. We also used to spend a lot of time in the house with the girls. One day, Rita showed us the large sideboard in the front room where her mother kept the goodies, tins of biscuits, lemonade, sweets, and tinned fruit. "Stuff for the visitors", Rita said. The sideboard had three locked doors with three drawers over them. She had discovered that all she had to do was to take out a drawer, and she could then reach down to the goodies inside. When she pulled out a bar of chocolate she swore us to secrecy, and we were very happy to go along.

Sometimes Mrs Kelly asked us to stay for dinner. She always said we were a great help to her with the younger children. The lads were always very hungry when they came in from the fields for dinner. The food was always ready and I had never seen such a big pot of potatoes in my life, before or since. I couldn't believe that they would all be eaten at one meal. My memory of the dinner is that it was a very happy event, with plenty of meat and vegetables. After we had helped with the clean-up we headed for the loft. It had straw on the floor, and that is where we all sat. We talked, sang, and played games until it was time to go home.

We were supposed to be home before dark, and of course we had to go the long way home by road, because it was too late for the fields. Rita and some of the lads would walk part of the way with us, and it was only when they left us that we started to think about facing our mothers. They had threatened us several times that they would stop us from going altogether because we always stayed too late. Many, many times as we came up our road we could see the two mothers at one door. They got together because they were worried about us, and when we saw them together we knew we were in for it. After a good telling-off we were always sent straight to bed. Jean and I were able to wave goodnight at each other from the back bedroom windows.

We only had one bad fright coming home during the couple of years we walked from the farmhouse. We had stayed late and it was getting dark as we headed home. A man on a bike came up behind us, kept cycling around us, and saying things like "Two lovely girls like you shouldn't be on your own, you should come with me". Jean was always more sensible, and better than I was at getting out of trouble, and kept saying, "Don't speak! Don't look at him! I'll hit him with the milk pail if he comes near us". Thank God he didn't. He just cycled off.

Often, though, she was the cause of our trouble. Once, she invented a game. The two of us were to hold a mouthful of buttermilk, and the winner was the one who could hold it in her mouth the longest. We did this a lot on the way home, and this went on until we had only a small amount of milk left in the pails. I was worried, but Jean advised, "Sure we'll tell them that Mrs Kelly was short of buttermilk today".

I make brown bread every day like my mother did, and I often remember Kelly's farmhouse. It would be nice to go back there again, through the fields with Jean for the good buttermilk.

KIERAN DUNNE

THE PRIZE

It was Friday, October 19th 2012. I was alone at home, sitting comfortably in a warm room, watching the evening news. The first item concerned the Troika, our quarterly political tourists. Cosseted by the sleep-inducing surroundings, I had begun to nod off when I heard a reference to a County Cork Patrician missionary. This awakened my reflective sensitivities as I had been a pupil at the Patrician School in Mallow about seventy years ago. The news item covered the conferring of Honorary Doctorate of Philosophy, by Dublin City University, on the world-renowned athletics coach Patrician Brother Colm O'Connell. He had coached five Kenyan Olympic Gold Medallists, including a gold medal winner in the 2012 London Olympics. This mention of a very famous Patrician, and of athletics generally, brought my mind back to the Annual Patrician School Sports in Mallow in the summer of 1943. Then eleven years old, my participation in those sports was for me exciting, challenging and triumphant. Alas, it was also tinged with personal sadness.

I am not going to dwell on the grim realities of World War II that had by now gripped Ireland –the hardship and impoverishment that cast an air of gloom and despair. Rather, with far greater insight now than that of the carefree young lad of eleven years, I subconsciously acknowledged the self-sacrificing and altruistic input of the local community towards easing the prevalent despondency. Low cost fixtures were frequently arranged, such as inter-street athletics competitions, feisanna, concerts and sales of work. As far as I was concerned, the main attraction would be the Annual Patrician School Sports in which I and older members of the family participated. Local businesses donated prizes. However, the donation of a prize, if affordable, would also be expected from individual families.

The question of a prize created a big problem for my family –money was scarce and demands were high. However, as three of us were participating, my mother, always a proud woman, felt that she should be among the subscribers. Resorting to her Emergency thinking, she studied the items displayed in a locked glass cabinet in our sitting room. To her, and indeed to my father, these were precious pieces of varied designs –china, silver, glass, and porcelain– no doubt most of sentimental value, that had survived the destructive tendencies of their eight children. She studied three items, a silver butter dish, a cut glass vase, and what we called a biscuiteer.

She brought the silver dish and the vase to the kitchen and washed them in sudsy water in the enamel basin. Having dried and shined these as best she could, she placed them on the table and studied them from various angles. Then, with a sigh, she placed them back in the sitting room cabinet. Later that evening, I overheard her say to my father, resignedly, that she'd have to give her cherished biscuiteer, as despite her best efforts, the other items did not look new. The biscuiteer was perfect and had never been used. It was an unusual and colourful piece of porcelain about nine inches high, complete with cover, embossed with BISCUITS and with very attractive intricate designs. My father put his arm around her shoulder and whispered "try not to worry – tis alright Annie, you have no option". Yes, she would submit it to the Sports Committee.

For a few days prior to the Sports, the washing board and ironing board withstood the constant scrubbing and pressing of white shorts and shirts. Canvas shoes resting outside on the windowsill were a dazzling white. Homemade colourful flags for the drill display rested beside them.

The big day arrived. The sun shone brightly. The Thomas Davis Pipe Band played rousing marching tunes. Bunting and little tricolours elaborately decorating the park's railings fluttered in the gentle breeze. Crackly announcements emanated from the loudspeakers. The public, parents and children, thronged the viewing areas, vying for the most advantageous position.

Digging deep in my ragbag of memories, I now relate, insofar as possible, details of my experience on that special day. I am to participate in three races –the three-legged race, the sack race and the

220 yards sprint. My past record in the three-legged race and the sack race is dismal –in the former, my shoe fell off and it tumbled both of us. In the sack race, my shorts fell down and crippled my efforts. I look forward especially to the 220 yards as I am a good sprinter.

3.30 pm. Next race, the 220 yards, is announced. Myself and eight other boys get on our marks –Jimmy, whom I fear most, is in the lane next to me. At the sound of the starter's gun and the shouts of spectators, the taut finishing tape is our aim. As it beckons, Jimmy and myself, neck and neck, turn the last bend. Arms and legs, like newly-greased pistons, work in unison, as we now approach the tape. A dead heat is the verdict –we must both compete again at 4.30 pm.

The designated time arrives. I stumble slightly at take-off but quickly regain my balance. I am now inching up on Jimmy. Renewed determination and effort propel me on in the last 20 yards. I breast the tape by a hair's breadth margin over my battling opponent. I have won.

It is now late evening. Awarding of prizes is at an advanced stage. I observe the biscuiteer still on the prizes table. Jimmy and I wait anxiously. I glimpse my mother among the onlookers –no doubt she is hoping, that by a stroke of luck her Kieran might retrieve her much loved biscuiteer.

Prize winners for the rerun of the 220 yard sprint is now signalled and the vital announcement emanates from the loudspeaker:

"Prize for first place: Kieran is awarded the beautiful blue cut-glass framed clock and candlesticks."

"Prize for second place: Jimmy is awarded the magnificent porcelain biscuiteer."

It was the first time in my life that I was sorry that I had been first.

BRIGID MURPHY

THE PARK RANGER'S DAUGHTER

On a recent visit to Phoenix Park I thought I would take a walk around an area I used to know very well. It has been many years since I visited the place, and it holds many memories for me.

I drove in through the North Circular Road entrance, past the white painted entrance gates. The Gate Lodge where the Caseys lived had a small area to the side where bicycles could be left for the day. Alongside that was the large grey building which houses the married quarters for the Gardaí stationed in the Garda headquarters. The lovely Victorian People's Gardens were on my left hand side. On past the Garda headquarters and McKee Barracks, with on the left hand side the Dublin Zoo with its myriad buildings and high forbidding fencing which blocks my view of the interesting sights that I know are behind it. I parked my car on the roadside close to the elephant enclosure and turned left onto Spa Road. I walked along this narrow road with double yellow lines either side warning people not to park there. I passed through the bollards preventing access by cars. On my left I came to the entrance of a building I know only too well. It is a two storey, semi-detached lodge, with grey walls and Virginia creeper clinging to it. The autumn leaves are long gone and the walls look bleak and bare. The house where the Kavanaghs lived looks neglected with the garden overgrown. Although old Mrs Kavanagh died a few years ago, it would appear the Office of Public Works don't intend to allocate her lodge again. Beside it is the house where I grew up, now inhabited by an elderly couple who have lived there since my family moved out. I stood at the gate for a few minutes looking up the pathway to the house and remembering my childhood and what life was like in that house many years ago.

My father and mother had moved into Spa Lodge in 1944 when Dad was appointed as a Park Ranger. The house was provided with the job. You walked in the narrow gate and up the pathway to the front door which was a double door, painted green, and opened onto a hallway that ran widthways. At one end of the hall was the kitchen/living room. It was a large square room with a black range in an alcove. There were two deep set windows with window sills about 3 ft deep, one on either side of the room. The windows were so large that a child could easily stand upright on the sills. At the other end of the hall was a parlour and several small rooms, including a kitchenette, a scullery and a larder. The larder had lots of shelves where all the dried food was stored. In the 1940s fridges were unheard of and food had to be stored in a cold area. Meat was stored in a container with fine mesh covering it to allow cold air to circulate while keeping out flies.

The parlour had a lovely black fireplace with green tiles inset down the sides. There was also a small black fireplace in each of the upstairs bedrooms.

The rooms were lit by gaslight which hung from the ceiling. This consisted of a metal frame with a white globe and inside that a delicate mantle. Two chains hung from the frame. One you pulled when lighting the mantle and the other when putting out the light.

The house had a large garden which was surrounded by a green painted wrought iron paling. Outside this was a very large green area which in summer time was used by people for picnics and for children to play on. In the garden there was an old Bramley apple tree which was a prolific producer of plenty of lovely, big apples, and for many years. There was also an old water pump but no matter how hard you pumped the handle, no water came out.

As a Park Ranger my Dad wore a uniform, not unlike a Garda's, with a peaked hat and brass buttons, which had to be polished every week. The smell of Brasso would linger in the air when the job was done.

The Park Rangers were allocated certain areas in the Park which they had to patrol and report on any problems they encountered. They had powers of arrest within the Park and if they came across anybody damaging shrubbery or causing a disturbance, etc. they could arrest the individual and have him charged. In those years they used bicycles to cover their designated areas.

There are less than 40 lodges in the Park. Some of these are gate lodges at the numerous entrances to the Park and the remainder are scattered throughout the Park. During the war years and for a number of years afterwards the main road in the Park, Chesterfield Road, had large mounds of turf stacked on either side of the road.

As young children, my sister and I had plenty of other children to play with. Children liked to come to our house as there was so much space. We went to school with some of the children living in the Garda married quarters and they often came to our house to play.

Before the garda training unit moved to Templemore it was based at Garda headquarters in Phoenix Park. Several times a week the young recruits would march along Spa Road past our house whistling a tune to which they marched in time.

Eventually the green area surrounding the house was taken over by the Zoo and a new elephant house was built and an aviary, along with facilities for some other animals. We could see into the elephant enclosure from our bedroom window and watch their keeper, Mr Kenny, tending to them. The paling around the house was the boundary line and it was very easy for us to get across it and go for a wander around the Zoo. However, we weren't allowed to do this very often.

The OPW painted the lodges every seven years. In those days everything was done to last. The lower half of the walls would be painted in a gloss finish and the upper half was matt. After a storm if any trees had fallen or become dangerous and needed to be felled, they would be cut up and distributed among the families living in the Park.

The people in the house adjoining ours were Barney and Janey Kavanagh. Barney was also a Park Ranger. He was a tall, good looking man and looked very good in his uniform. They had three children, two boys and a girl who were some years older than us and we admired them greatly. Ann was lovely looking and she became a fashion model. Sometimes we were invited into their house to see Ann before she set off for a fashion show or function. She always looked very glamorous. Brian started off his working life as an egg salesman and he spent hours in the shed checking eggs to make sure they were fresh by holding them up to a light which shone right through them. He was ambitious and moved on to greater things in later life.

Once there was an alarm raised when a monkey escaped from the Zoo. The Park Rangers and other workers were galvanised into action to search for the animal. Occasionally we had the odd exotic bird fly into the garden and for years we had some magnificent tail feathers that they dropped.

At all times of the year, Phoenix Park was a popular place for people to walk, run and cycle in. During winter time when snow was on the ground the Magazine Fort drew people, young and not so young, to toboggan down the steep slopes surrounding it. The slopes were quite long so you got a good, fast run. Everything was used from well-made sleds to trays to pieces of wood with strips of tin nailed on the underside to give speed. Dad had made a wooden sled for us with strips of tin nailed on the underside. Two children could sit on it. It was a good sled and we ourselves and some of our friends had good fun racing down the hill and trying to avoid crashing into some of the others.

We were friendly with the children who lived in the Phoenix Cricket Club. Their living accommodation was part of the Club premises and their Dad looked after the Cricket grounds. They were the same age as us. As a child I found the Cricket Club a little spooky as some of the rooms were very large and hollow sounding when you walked across the wooden floors. There were pictures of past members hanging on the walls which gave the rooms a sombre air.

When my father resigned from his job and went to England to work, we had to vacate the house in the Park. However, the OPW were generous to us and allowed us to remain in the house for a considerable period of time.

When we left, the OPW updated the house for the new family. They removed the range and replaced the gas lighting with electricity for the new family moving in. These modern fittings were essential but I will always remember the lodge as it used to be with its black range and the soft gaslight and candlelight which illumed my childhood.

MY BROTHER DERMOT

I was the seventh child in a family of nine, and from a very young age I realised how lucky I was to have five older brothers. In many ways they had a huge influence on my life, almost all of it for the better.

One or two of them were always at the dances in the local hall, and I made them promise not to desert me, and to get me on the dance floor early. That gave me an advantage with their friends as the night went on. I didn't know what being a wallflower felt like until I was without them. They would also cover for me with my parents if I was out later than I was supposed to be. When I was about fifteen I stayed overnight with a school friend in a nearby town. We both sneaked out to an adult dance that I knew was very seriously out of bounds. To my surprise my oldest brother was there with his girlfriend, and he was equally surprised to see me. I got some eldest-brother advice, but he kept my secret, and never told my mother, or anybody else that I had been there.

I have very strong memories of many family events, but because four of my brothers left Ireland to work in America or England, and settled in these countries, it changed family life in many different ways. They emigrated over a number of years, which had a huge impact on me. I hated the build-up during the weeks before a brother left the house. We all knew what was happening, but no one wanted to talk about it, especially my mother. It seemed to have always had the same crying sadness, loneliness, and just loss of the things we were all part of.

Dermot was the youngest brother, just two years older than me, and we were very close. He was a caring, good-humoured, and a fun person to be with. Sometimes, of course, he could be too much fun. Any time I took myself too seriously I could be sure that he would be the first to puncture my self-importance. It's only with hindsight that I realise how unusual he was for a country boy in those days. He loved nature, and would draw my attention to things like the colour of the leaves; the first snowdrops peeping through the cold ground, and lying flat on the grass, watching for pinkeens in a stream. From about the time that he was fourteen years old he carried a pocket-sized edition of Omar Khayyam, and took every opportunity to stand in front of me, holding me captive, while reading this poetry that made no sense to me at all.

We called him 'the bear-hug brother' because he constantly crept behind my sisters and me at the most inconvenient moments, and put his arms around us so tightly that he would squeeze the breath out of us. We usually protested loudly but he only laughed at us. He himself, however, was like a breath of warm air whenever we were with him.

The day he left for England it seemed a huge weight had come down on the house, and you couldn't get away from it. It was the first time I heard my mother crying out loud. I remember how disturbed I was listening to her. As children we used to call it a 'heg in your heart' –that involuntary sound you made after you had cried a lot.

Dermot played the accordion well and he loved to play waltzes. On the day he left he spent the last hour in his bedroom playing more plaintive tunes than waltzes and these only increased our own sadness. I can remember only two of the tunes now. One was 'The Chualain', and the other was 'I'll Take You Home Again Kathleen', that hackneyed, but still very sad tune about a woman who could never overcome her homesickness. I have no doubt at all that I would be like poor Kathleen. The idea of living my life abroad, in another country, always filled me with dread.

None of us looked at each other while the music filled the house, we were all just thinking of him leaving. We knew he had a heavy heart too, and though we had often teased him about his playing, particularly when he was learning a new tune, we were secretly proud of his ability. He couldn't take his accordion with him because it was too big to put in his luggage, and he would have to leave it behind. We knew this broke his heart.

When he had finished playing, the house suddenly became so silent that we could hear him putting away the accordion. Nobody could talk. Then we heard him coming down the stairs. He stopped at the door of the kitchen; my mother was furiously poking the fire with her back to him. She could not look at him. I knew that she was trying to keep herself together. He said to her,

"Will you not say goodbye to me?"

Being the youngest boy Dermot spent a lot of time with my father. They both loved fishing and gardening, and they had many trips to the local bog together to cut turf. I often went with them for a day out, and to make the tea. My father was a garda, and on the day Dermot left he was on duty in the barracks. He just said a quick goodbye to him before he left for work, and it is only now, looking back, that I'm sure he had arranged to be on duty that day. He had taken the easy way out —he just couldn't bear to be in the house.

His lovely son, with an Honours Leaving Cert, could not get a job. The only work he got was as a substitute teacher to fill in a few times for a teacher who was ill. He was also on a waiting list for the County Council Office, but he knew the list was too long, so he made the decision to go. Ireland lost a beauty in my lovely brother. Strangely enough, he never bought, or played another accordion after that.

A MISCELLANY OF GHOSTS

Lorcan, our eldest brother, along with his pal Bobby Dow, would put down night lines in the river and they were often lucky, providing us with trout for breakfast. Bobby? He was an only son and consequently was a bit spoiled by his elder sisters and parents. He was also a burly built chap; his head was unusually round, his shoulders were round, giving him an over-weight appearance. He lived with his family in a lovely little cottage in Swords down by the river.

Bobby's father was a lifer in the British army and I'm sure quite busy at that time, it being 1942, he came home occasionally and after a day or two would be gone again. Bobby was a loner, a little abandoned in that he attended the local Protestant school where there were few lads of his own age, so interface with others was a problem. His interest in football and hurling was non existent, as was ours at the time, we having no football or other kids to play with. Bobby began to visit of an evening, joining us in the woods to gather kindling. He would slowly climb the odd tree then strut around as if he'd climbed Everest. The same tree we'd shin up in a minute. He claimed he was expert at everything, as any thirteen or fourteen year olds do.

He had a throwing knife this particular evening, a knife he'd fashioned himself. During his long, loud and detailed description of how he nearly killed a rabbit and which entailed him waving this knife about, the blade flew out and stuck fast between my barefooted toes and into the root of a tree. It never drew a drop of blood. Instead of relieved apologies, the dope began to brag he'd aimed to obtain this result. We were not amused.

Another evening, our father was working in the garden with a few of the lads including Sean Moylan, leaning over the fence chatting, when Bobby happens along. Without being asked he announced he was an expert gardener. Our father in devilment asked him was he any good to fight? Bobby took the bait and stated he was an expert boxer. "You'd never beat Sean" our father proposed. Sean, a blocky lad and a year or two older than Bobby but with the arms of a blacksmith, smirked at the prospect. The fight began immediately with Sean giving Bobby a clout in the gob which knocked him over. Bobby, in tears, gamely got to his feet and said it was not fair, so Sean gave him another. By this time our mother, alerted by the cheers of Sean's supporters rushed out to rescue him and to also give our father an earful and the lads their walking papers. Bobby was then brought inside and mollified with a mug of hot tea and several scones until proceedings were interrupted by a knock on the door. It was a delegation of the lads offering their profuse apologies and announced that Sean too was terrible sorry for giving Bobby a "sly one". So, after further admonishment by our mother, Bobby's prestige was restored and the lads rehabilitated.

Our mother had always liked Bobby, mainly because he was so polite, particularly at table, such as "Could I have another slice of tart Mrs Redmond", or "may I have another scone, another cup of tea". We liked Bobby too for he was non-threatening, and only came to the woods to live out his dreams.

His mother was a lovely little person, bespectacled and always smiling. She was also extremely talented. As a confectioner she had no equal, indeed, when invited to little parties in their cottage, where we were the only guests, we cleaned her out of her delectable tiny sweet-meats, her featherweight pancakes with their wild honey filling. Then tea in china cups –cups with handles and saucers! Her prowess as a seamstress was illustrated in the magnificent patchwork quilts and cushion covers about her sitting room and bedrooms. The combination of colours, fabrics and geometrical patterns were absolute works of art. God! I so envy and admire those Mrs Dows of the world, who quietly and unassumingly can give voice to their soul. For several years Bobby was part of our lives –indeed, enriched by them until circumstance left us living where our paths did not cross. Bobby eventually married and became verger of St Columba's Swords, living in the lodge. Poor Bobby died a few years ago, may he rest in peace.

Three of the O'Tooles from Swords, Cles, Cahaill, and Johnny, were also excellent fishermen who frequented the lakes and river. There were others who came to hunt —one fellow to ferret for rabbits. Another group to shoot —that's when they got the "Billy" that the "Big Fella", the estate owner was away. They would wheel their bicycles through the wicket gate situated at the end of our house and park them in the shade. Our mother, on hearing the squealing gate would invite them in for a cup of tea.

One incident regarding these hunters stands out. A Christian Brother, a myopic weedy little fellow wearing glasses, accompanied by a couple of others, turned up about twice a year. On this occasion, having being out shooting, he was in the highest of spirits as he took from his bag a most beautiful milk white bird with its neck feathers delicately tipped with gold. I remember it being about ten or twelve inches long as he proudly laid it on the table. He'd shot a golden owl, an extremely rare bird even in those days. His intention he told us was to have it stuffed and exhibited in his All Hallows college refectory. We thought it was him who should be stuffed. Anyway, it was a horrible thing to do. I've often wondered if it was the last of the species or are there still one or two meandering in the twilight down by the river.

There happened another incident of note around this time. I remember it being near the end of our holidays as my brother Frank and I were gathering kindling in the garlic covered woods. I was 8 and Frank was 4. Red Cloud, a native American Indian chief, and the title of a book which we had been reading in school, must have been on my mind when this super idea struck me. Why not camp here in the woods like the Indians? I sat down on the stump of a tree to ponder on the concept and couldn't find one negative reason as to why not. I don't remember consulting Frank for his advice or opinion, or dwelt for an instant on whatever opinions our parents might have on the subject but immediately engaged myself in selecting a camp site. The spot I chose was nearby, and remote from casual strollers. It was where two ancient walls met at right angles, the area surrounded by dense elder and Elm trees. Of course a camp must have a fire, so I raced home the four minute trot to where Lorcan was sawing timber into blocks as well as minding our infant brother Billy —our mother being away milking and father away working. Furtively, I secured a couple of matches and sequestered two empty tins —well, we needed cups. I then returned to the camp where we got a great fire going. As I busied myself making the camp snug I decided for continuity; I would train Frank to be a soldier.

Should we need supplies we could borrow from Mrs Shields who lived on their farm three hundred yards away, or from Mrs Dooley who lived three hundred yards in the opposite direction. Most of our food would be foraged from the "Big Fella's" hen house, apples from his orchard and the remainder from George Naylor's strawberry beds.

When engaged in these momentous plans and decisions, half the district's population were out looking for us —especially around the lakes and river. As it grew darker and the resident Jackdaws were settling, I deemed it time to make the beds. While in the process of gathering moss and leaves we heard somebody climbing the wall, it was our father. "What the bloody hell d'ya think you're doin' here?" he bellowed as he stamped out the fire. "You're in for it when you get home", he emphasised with a shake of his head –climbing back over the wall to his bicycle.

Yes, I got it right enough but being used to it I don't remember, and only regretted that but for our father cycling down the Brackenstown road and getting the whiff of wood smoke the North County Dublin could have had its own Red Cloud.

KAY PHILPOTT

THE OLD SEWING MACHINE

In the 1940's needlework material was hard to come by, and the nuns in our Convent School used to dole out tiny pieces of linen or cotton about four or five inches square, on which to practise our stitches in Sewing Class. Thread they rationed to a length of about ten inches per person and this was often reduced considerably by our damping and clipping the ends in an effort to get it through the tiny eye of the needle. Many grubby efforts at top-sewing, hemming or "run-and-fell" seams were presented for Sister's caustic comments, and as we grew older, the dreaded button-holes were often meted out as a punishment for misdemeanours. You kept working till you got it straight —and neat. I longed to be able to stitch them on my aunt's sewing machine.

That machine was part of my youth. My mother's housekeeping skills covered unsurpassed mothering, exceptional cooking, adequate knitting, but definitely not dressmaking. Her older unmarried sister,

Aunt Mary, on the other hand, loved "making" for her small nieces. She must have bought the machine in the 1920's when she became the family housekeeper after my grandmother's death. She used it for purposes both functional and recreational. From an early age, I remember watching, fascinated, as she removed the tubular cover exposing its mysteries, checked the oil, deftly threaded the various holders, filled the bobbin and finally pulled two matching ends of thread towards her. Then the two pieces of material to be stitched were carefully aligned –and the whole apparatus lowered on to it.

Summer dresses in bright shades of blue, pink, green or lemon, winter skirts heavily pleated in wool or tartan and always with a bodice attached, as befitted children's skirts in those days, single breasted coats with velvet collars, all were turned out on time and in season. I don't really remember adult garments of my aunt's making, although I'm sure she kept herself and her sisters well supplied. As I grew older I'm afraid I lost interest and developed a teenager's horror of appearing in public in a "home-made" outfit. I never did learn to manipulate that machine, although I later mastered an electric model when my own children were small.

My aunt grew old along with her machine which was tucked away in a corner, its tubular lid rarely raised. When she died at the ripe old age of 92, I was surprised and touched to find she had left the Singer to me. I, in turn, found a corner for it in my living-room and wondered to what use it could be put. The lid still lifted easily to reveal parts as bright as ever. The little drawer underneath the bobbin-holder contained a treasury of reels of thread, pins, needles, buttons, a crochet-hook and a little can of oil.

It sat there for some years but now, once more, it has come into its own. When my son and his family moved into their house in Wexford a few years ago, he asked if I would pass on the machine to them. I wondered if its days of fulfilling its owners' creative instincts were over. But I need not have worried. Last time I visited, there it was in all the glory of a conversation piece – a thoroughly modern telephone table!

LIFE LESSONS

What has living this life taught me?
Are we destined to plod the same paths our fathers did
Reaching out for our destiny only to find it turn to dust?

Mistakes teach, not life.
Life is the breeze against your face, the soft rain touching your brow
The joy of childish hugs and kisses for your grandchildren.

Remembering days before, of relieve-i-o, broken statues, chasing.
And football in the field –"it's my ball, you're not playing".
This from a boy who became a man with a limp handshake.

Kissing up the lane and going home red-faced, wondering
Does it show. "You're late, where were you?"
The mammy worries, yet is glad you are safe.

School was different. No games, no girls, only gaelic and hurling.
Slaps for soccer, slaps for lates, slaps for ecker.
And unholy touches from holy men.

It didn't do me any harm.

And then the job —yes, sir, no sir, at once sir.
No biffs here, only hard work and long hours.
Money for the boss, the ma and a little for myself.

Then the sweet times. The love of my life.
Courting in the old-fashioned way, engagement
And marriage —wonderful, fairytale time.

Highs and lows, but mostly highs. The perfect partner.
With total trust. We looked after each other.
But it was not for life, not for my life anyway.

What has life taught me?
Very little it seems —I still make the same mistakes.
I still trust people until they displace that trust.

Out of duty, out of habit, I go to family functions,
Not liking to say no, not wanting to be awkward,
Not knowing if I'd be missed.

And somehow, I know, I won't be.

ARLENE MCALLISTER

TRAUMA ON THE SKI SLOPES

It was on the 8th of March 1966, the day Nelson's Pillar in O'Connell St. was blown up, that I too had a most traumatic experience.

When I was in my 20's I used to go skiing every year. After about eight trips, I was getting quite good at it. It was a super holiday and a great getaway from a hectic career.

My friends and I travelled to Austria mostly, visiting places such as Westendorf, Kirchberg, Ehrwald, and Innsbruch. As soon as we arrived in one of the many picturesque villages, we immediately felt at home; we always found the Austrians to be kind and friendly. The first sight of the wonderful soft snow –not like the awful wet substance we get here– would lift our hearts. My memory is of sunshine during the day and really cold nights and early mornings, big open fires and friends sitting around chatting and drinking hot chocolate or sometimes Gluwein –warm wine with special spices added– after a strenuous day on the slopes. Austrian food is wholesome and delicious and it was here that I was introduced to sauerkraut –a vegetable dish with cabbage as its base. Each morning, we headed for the slopes in our heavy ski boots and our skis on our shoulders. The glare from the sun on the snow was so bright, it would blind you. We walked past the various hotels with their duvets hanging out the windows to air. The fresh air was intoxicating.

One year we went to Kitzbuhl and on the second day of our trip, I was invited to join another more experienced group. They were heading for the top of the huge Hannenkamm mountain range. I loved the idea of being asked and was looking forward to the challenge.

At 6.30 am the following morning we set off for the chair lifts. The only sound to be heard in the silence was the crunch of our boots on the soft snow. It took three stations on the chair lifts to reach the summit and look out over the valley; you could see for hundreds of miles and the air was so crisp and clear.

At the top of the mountain we had breakfast in the coffee shop. Muesli, fresh fruit and piping hot coffee were served to us by a rather rotund middle aged man who had a ruddy complexion and a great sense of humour even at that hour of the morning! At 9.30 am we commenced our descent, traversing right and left and over hills and avoiding trees. It was exhilarating and we were looking forward to spending the day descending to the base of this mountain range.

Then all of a sudden it happened —the tip of my left ski went into a pot hole. The sound of the crack was ear splitting. I went flying through the air and landed badly. I was in great pain. Luckily there were two doctors in our group, young Germans who had just qualified. Tall, elegant guys, they were the athletic types. One of them lit a cigarette and pushed it into my mouth. I'd never had a cigarette before! The other one sat beside me and held my hand before he explained that I had broken my leg badly. In fact I had broken my tibia —the big centre bone of my left leg. But he also explained that I was lucky that the bone had not protruded the skin. I didn't feel lucky!

Meanwhile the ski instructor was trying to contact the rescue people and the rest of our group were frozen standing around waiting for almost an hour for help to arrive. It came in the form of a stretcher and two ambulance men. I screamed with pain as they strapped up my leg and tied me very tightly onto the stretcher with several blankets because I was shivering with shock and fear at this stage. Then we took off —one of them at my head and the other at my feet. Down this huge mountain I went at great speed with these two expert skiers. It was such a pity that I was in so much pain, I was unable to enjoy the experience!

Next stop was the ambulance and then the local GP. He was a crotchety man of about fifty and my memory of him is that he was rather dismissive —probably because he was used to seeing several broken limbs in any one day. We then made the nineteen mile trip to the hospital in St Johann. It was a large, very modern orthopaedic hospital. It had two helicopter landing pads which were for difficult rescues. The nurses and doctors were very kind and gentle with me. In the hospital theatre my clothes were cut off and my leg was put into plaster from the top of my leg to my toes. I was then brought down several corridors on a trolley and all I could see were dozens of people with legs, arms and even fingers in plaster. The ward where I was brought to was a large room with several very big oval windows. Each evening the moon shone on the top of the snow clad mountain which we could see from our beds. It was so tranquil to watch it and in the end this image helped us to sleep in this foreign environment.

There were three of us in the ward, and the other girls had similar problems to mine. One of the girls was Austrian and the other one was from New Zealand. In those days our broken legs were held on a pulley and hung from the ceiling. Once the plaster was applied, my pain subsided somewhat but not altogether. I still had moments of severe pain. My pidgin German and the Austrian girls' bit of English helped us to communicate well, in between some awful pain. The New Zealander had a guitar and she played and sang some beautiful Maori songs. Sometimes others joined us from across the corridor. Every day at lunch time a brass band set up in the Square outside the hospital and played umpah, umpah type of music for about an hour –very uplifting. The Austrian girl was married and her husband and baby would come in to see her, daily. The New Zealander and I had few visitors but we got to know each other and kept in touch for several years afterwards. She ended up teaching P.E. in Portugal and she married a Portuguese policeman whom she met at traffic lights in Lisbon one day.

Each morning this nun, the one who used to wear the big bonnets, would come into our ward. She would remove all our clothing and leave us there 'starkers' with our legs hanging from the ceiling. Then she would go and get each of us a basin of hot water and place it onto our stomachs and order us to 'vash'. She was a tall, slim and elegant woman who made no effort to communicate with any of the three of us. Her long deep blue habit made her look taller. But I wondered how much starch had to be used to make her white bonnet stand up in two peaks at either side of her head! All she cared about were her plants which she talked to. They were in the corner of our ward.

At this point, every day, the newspaper man would come in. He was a jolly sort of man in his 40's. He wore a green alpine jacket with a pleat down the back and a tweed hat with a little feather in it. He had a bundle of newspapers tucked under his arm. I was first inside the door and would shout at him to 'get out', since the three of us were naked and trying to wash ourselves. His reply was always the same, "no problem, sure I am married!". He would present each of us with our newspaper and await payment. Meanwhile the nun who was over at the window, watering her plants and singing away to herself, never once tried to come to our aid! He would say "guten morgen" to her each day, but he never got a reply.

About eight days into this regimen, an x-ray was required to check how my leg was healing in the plaster. The Hungarian surgeon who was a short, dark haired, kind hearted man, informed me in his broken English that my leg was crooked in the plaster and that it would have to be 're-arranged'. What this meant was that an electric saw was required to work its way through the plaster so that at some point the plaster could be twisted and therefore my leg would be straightened. He said "when it touches your skin you tell me!". I thought he was joking, until he carved a circle right around the plaster and I could feel the tickle as the saw touched my skin a few times. Thank goodness, it worked but unfortunately my ankle was left at an angle and has caused me huge problems ever since.

After two weeks, it was time to fly home to Dublin. I got a first class seat on the plane which was one of the old Viscounts with the propellers. I was heavily sedated. About half way home I was looking out the window of the plane and I saw one of the engines had stopped. A few minutes later a second one stopped. We were now out over the Irish Sea and so I pulled down the blind and said to myself that if we were going down, I didn't want to see it! A short time later the Captain told us that he had lost two engines and that he was going to fly into Dublin manually. We arrived home only forty minutes late, and I lived to tell the tale!

At Dublin Airport, I was put onto the carousel with all the baggage until a wheelchair could be found for me. Back in a Dublin hospital the doctors were very cautious because it was such a bad break and they kept me in the plaster for four months and a half. They were very impressed with the way my leg was set in the plaster in Austria and in fact took several photos of it. In Ireland in the 1960's, limbs were still plastered in a big lump, while my plaster was neat and shaped around my leg. The doctors here had never seen anything like it.

I went back skiing the following year, somewhat in fear and trepidation, but I made the decision to start from the beginning again and I learnt from scratch in the nursery class. In the end, my fears were in vain and I thoroughly enjoyed another wonderful skiing holiday.

MICHAEL O'SULLIVAN

A FUNERAL AND ITS SEQUEL

We are near the city of Waterford, having driven from Dublin in the morning, in sunny summer weather, which is anything but the right backdrop for the event that has prompted our trip. The occasion is a sad one. It is the funeral of an elderly lady well known to us and always well liked. We are not shocked by her death, but definitely surprised. She was in the autumn of life, but not in the bracket of a near departure.

Our connection is through her son, an extremely close friend. We reflect how sad the situation must be for him; there is a normal sorrow in the passing of any close relation, but the final parting from the one who carried and nurtured you for almost a year before you were put on this earth, tugs most severely on the heartstrings.

Now we stand in a small rural ivy-clad church with an adjoining cemetery. Our dark Sunday best suits blend perfectly with the already gathered congregation, some whispering condolences, waiting for the requiem mass to begin. Softened coughs grow silent as we stand for the arrival of the celebrant on the altar. The death liturgy proceeds, interspersed with familiar solemn and prayerful hymns, including the favourite 'Ag Criost an siol'. Grandchildren, with unusually serious faces, play their part, taking leads in the prayers of the faithful and bringing gifts up to the altar. The ceremony comes to a close, with a homily by one of the family, followed by final prayers. Then, the coffin is carried shoulder-high to the adjoining graveyard and the open gravesite. Margaret Carey, RIP, is quietly laid to rest. We remain in the graveyard for a respectful period, as we sympathise with Margaret's relatives, and are particularly attentive to her son, our very close friend.

How quickly the scene is changed. No trace of sadness. There is a buzz of happy voices, helped by a fine meal, wine and other drink, as the customary post-funeral reception gathers pace. Reminiscences about the departed abound, especially those which provoke hearty laughter. Her good qualities, spiced with some of her eccentricities, are on every tongue. All are agreed that she is gone 'to a better place'. Once again the clock seems to have accelerated; it is time for us to start our homeward journey. We repeat our sympathies, thank our hosts for their generous hospitality, and speed off towards distant Dublin.

As we journey on, we realise that we are somewhat more affected than we would have thought by the liquid hospitality. Simultaneously, we agree that we should break our return trip. A moment's thought suggests a nearby hotel, well known to us, where we have enjoyed many a visit.

What a contrast in scene greets us as we arrive. This is a wedding reception, in full swing. Meal over, a lively band leaves us with no doubt about the dominant mood. We take our seats on the edge of the dance floor, to which we ferry our drinks, and we study the gathering. We have arrived at a point which will be very familiar to anyone who was ever at a wedding in Ireland. The men are following the tradition of fortifying themselves at the bar before they venture on to the dance floor. The ladies, young and not-so-young, are seated around the dance area, using conversation to hide their frustration. We feel as if we had arrived like wolves on a fold without a shepherd in sight! Without a moment's hesitation, we decide to become uninvited guests, and head confidently towards the female array. Did we delude ourselves, or did we detect a sense of anticipation and joy coming over almost each, if not every face? We did not dwell on this too long, we were too busy dancing, doing our best to leave no one disappointed. We're those types of people. As they say, all good things come to an end, and so did this, eventually. Once more, we are on our interrupted journey.

This was uneventful and silent. A combination of the demon drink and tripping the light fantastic had, at last, got the better of a dough warrior and my companion had slipped into the land of Nod from which he did not emerge until the car stopped in front of his home.

The day in question I will never forget, and here you may observe that I revert to the singular. Why so? My great friend and companion has no recollection whatsoever of our stop at that attractive hotel! That's just his bad luck, that's life. But I can assure you that it did happen, and that what I have recorded is the truth, the whole truth and nothing but the truth.

MICHAEL MORRIS

GRANDAD'S PHILOSOPHY

I liked my Grandfather Joe. I liked him a lot.

Joe was my mother's father and he'd had a pretty colourful life. He'd served in the Royal Munster Fusiliers during the Great War, spent some time in a concentration camp and then came home to face two years in Leopardstown sanatorium being treated for post-traumatic trauma, or shell-shock as they called it then.

After that he spent some time working on building sites in Dublin, some of which included The Theatre Royal and the West Cabra housing development. He then went to England and spent most of his remaining working life there because jobs for ex-British servicemen in Ireland were scarce on the ground.

He was working in London when I was born. Of course, I don't remember that, but my father tells me that because I was born the day after St Patrick's Day and the day before my grandfather's birthday, Joe told him I had brought my name home with me. My own father, who didn't like being dictated to and was always ahead of his time, told him in no uncertain terms that the woman who gave birth to me would name me. And so I was named after my father and my father's father.

The first time I remember meeting Joe was while back on holiday in London at six years of age. He greeted us getting off the train in Euston Station. I still have an image of this tall man with a definite military bearing about him, striding down the platform.

At this stage he would come home only for festive times as a lot of Irish did then, but in 1951 after an almighty row in the family and a subsequent separation, he departed again to England. About six years later he got his English pension and decided to come home for good. Because of the separation he lived with us for a couple of years until my grandmother decided he had mellowed enough in his old age, and took him back into the family home.

Personality-wise he was an extremely funny man, always quick with the quips and with a ready wit. He had brought back many songs from his army days and he would readily sing them without any urging at the Saturday night knees-ups, which occurred regularly. His dark side wasn't seen so much then as when he was younger —that was when he solved any problems with his fists. Many of my uncles when they were younger were recipients of this crude justice when they encountered his displeasure. And so did my grandmother. His daughters blamed the violence on his war experiences and said he came back a changed man. But many of his five sons had very little time for him, and all of them had served in the British or Irish forces.

As a grandson I felt privileged when I was older to be able to have an occasional pint with him. I liked the fact that he didn't use bad language, or soldiers' talk, as he called it. He was always good company and I enjoyed his conversation in the pub. This usually took place in Downey's on the Cabra Road, where he had a regular pew. My father was always with me on these occasions. The pints flowed at a good pace usually, though being quite inexperienced, I could never keep pace with them.

He spoke, and we listened. My dad, who was usually quite talkative and forthright, generally concentrated on his pint while Grandad was talking. He spoke of his time in England, working on the building sites and about the people he met; he spoke about not really mixing with the Irish over there, because he thought they were too hot-tempered and too ready to have a fight. He never spoke about his time in the British Army during the Great War. I tried to draw him out on it, but he always changed the subject, except once to say to me that he never wanted to join the army but he had to feed his family. There was no work for him in Dublin.

One time the conversation turned to discipline in the home. I will never know how the pub talk turned in this direction, but I do recall that at one stage Grandad leaned over to me and said "a man has a right to beat his wife; it says so in the Bible".

I sat impassively, not knowing what to think, and seeing this man whom I idolised crumble before my eyes off the pedestal I had built for him. My face, hopefully, didn't betray my emotions, my disgust at what he said. I heard him out, partly in deference to him being my elder and my revered grandfather. I listened and didn't comment, out of respect for him. After all, I reasoned, he came from an era that condoned that sort of thing. How I kept my feelings hidden remain a mystery to me to this day, but eventually he turned, or I turned, the conversation to something else.

At this stage my illusions were shattered. This was a man whom I thought had the highest ideals and suddenly, in one short sentence he had tumbled my thoughts upside down and inside out. I looked sideways at my father. He gave nothing away. His face was impassive. It betrayed no thoughts, no emotions. What was he thinking? My father had disciplined me as a boy, but I had never seen him raise his hand to my mother. Did he agree with those sentiments?

Because we'd had a few pints at this stage, Joe needed to go to the toilet. He got up and walked away unsteadily towards the back of the pub. As soon as he had gone, my father leaned towards me, without hesitation. He looked around, making sure that Grandad was out of earshot and nobody else was listening, and whispered to me, not gently, but defiantly, "Don't mind that oul' bastard".

ARLENE MCALLISTER

THE LAST DUET

"Figlia! —Mio Padre!"

"I'm afraid the news is not good", the neurologist said to my father. "You are suffering from motor neurone disease —you may survive for just about two years".

Those words hit all the family, particularly Dad, like a rocket. We had never heard of this disease and I was very unsure how Dad and I would deal with it. But I knew what I had to do; I had to put my life on hold for at least the next two years to look after him.

We had not seen eye to eye about many things over the years but we shared one passion; music, and more particularly opera. Music had always given both of us joy. At the age of twelve he had introduced me to the wonderful world of opera and we had enjoyed many performances together. Mam came too!

I had just purchased and moved into a new apartment about six months before we got this awful news. I had decorated it to suit my taste in pale pink and a lovely soft shade of green and I loved it. I had the most wonderful views of the Wicklow Hills from my kitchen window. Now I had to leave my cosy apartment and move back home to help my Dad to have some sort of quality of life for as long as possible.

I loved my family home and it had been difficult to make the decision to purchase a place of my own. Now I had to make the decision to move back home again. My emotions were up and down. But I concentrated on the job I felt I had to do. At the time, I had no idea that, due to unforeseen circumstances, I would never return to my pretty apartment.

Dad was not a tall man. He was about five feet six inches in height and despite his love of sweet things had managed to control his weight and was quite slim at this stage of his life. He had a round, full face and his hair was now a wonderful snowy white. He was always in good humour and looked happy −a great disposition. He was a smart dresser and wore suits during the working week and tweed jackets and casual trousers at the weekends. Dad had lived a very full, healthy and extremely busy life for many, many years and now at 73 years of age, he had just been handed a death sentence. I had no idea how he and I were going to deal with this awful news. Well, we cried first and when we were drained of tears, without discussing it, we decided to get on with the task of keeping Dad alive for just another couple of years. He had a wicked sense of humour and could usually laugh off most things, but this was something different. This had a finality to it.

Dad thrived on being busy. Running one's own business can be exhausting and utterly draining at times. He only slept about five hours a night and he was last to bed and first up every morning. Even on Saturdays and Sundays, he was up at cock crow, and ready to play golf with some of his many friends at Portmarnock Golf Club. My dear mother was often left alone with us kids, for the sake of a game of golf!

Mam had died two years before Dad received the bad news about his health. He was devastated and mourned her for a long time. She was a small, slightly-built woman, much loved by all five of us. She had dark brown hair, blue eyes and a winning smile and was kind and generous to a fault. She cared deeply for all of us. She was very ladylike and wore pretty dresses or skirts and twin-sets with pearls. Occasionally, she wore trousers. Mam had been a wife and mother and never worked outside the home. Every day there were hot meals on the table for us and new recipes to be tried out and never ever was there a crumb left on the plates! She had been living with a serious kidney complaint since she was 24. She went into hospital for a check-up and some respite and while there she had a stroke and so at the age of 66 she passed on, gently.

Towards the end of Mam's life, Dad started to complain of pains in the backs of his legs. As you would expect, at 73 years of age, the doctors first thought it was hardening of the arteries and treated it as such. But it was not long before a neurologist was recommended.

With heavy hearts, Dad and I commenced our new life together. We were like 'the odd couple' before this news, arguing about this and that, constantly! On reflection I think it was because we were so alike. But without saying a word to each other, we decided to make the most of any time that was left to us and we started to love one another.

I was working in the family business too, along with three of my four brothers. The fourth one escaped and worked for 'Uncle Arthur's Brewery'. Three of my brothers were married and bringing up their own families and the youngest one was living with Dad and me. I was trying to figure out how I could go to work and still look after my father, who was deteriorating before my eyes. I came up with a plan and it worked amazingly well. I stayed with Dad in the mornings and a wonderful neighbour very kindly offered to take care of him in the afternoons. When I returned home from the office at 6.30 pm each evening, I took over again.

Our schedule was difficult and kept changing as the disease progressed. First thing in the morning, I would wake up my father. He was propped up on at least five pillows to help him breathe. We always had a small night light on in the room for him because he was nervous of waking during the night and perhaps falling out of the bed. I slept in my room with one ear open and one asleep for all that period and if I thought he was having difficulties breathing, I would go in to him. Then I would lay him across the bed and thump his chest to improve his breathing. It worked after about twenty minutes. A local physiotherapist had kindly taught me how to do it.

His speech was one of the first things to go and so we had little slates everywhere in the house for him, so that he could communicate by writing down questions, his thoughts, jokes and how he was feeling etc., and then erase them. Yes, he had many jokes to tell me and in fact he was the one who kept me going during those two years. He was still able to wash and dress himself but I worked out a schedule with my brothers who would come and bathe him two or three times a week. After one such bath by one of my brothers, Dad emerged from the bathroom with a shiny red face and a glow all over. He wrote on his slate, "I feel as if I have been scrubbed with a Brillo Pad!". Indeed there were suds on the walls, the ceiling, and the floor —everywhere!

About sixteen months into the disease, he was getting physically weaker. Breakfast was an ordeal. It could take up to two hours to get one bowl of porridge and one slice of toast and a cup of tea into him because his throat muscles were deteriorating. A good family friend called most mornings and he would take over this job from me and so allow me to get on with other chores about the house. For example, I would set up a small table and light a candle in readiness for the local curate to call with Communion for Dad. This happened every day around noon. It was a wonderful peaceful time for Dad and he looked so spiritual as he said his prayers: close to God, I often thought.

I usually prepared dinner at lunch time, as it was easier for Dad to digest his food at this time of day. So when the meal was cooked, I would show him what we were having. For example something simple like chops, turnip and mash or chicken, carrots, peas and potatoes. Then I would liquidise his meal, so that he could swallow it more easily. He was happy once he saw what he was supposed to be eating because when food is liquidised, it looks like a dog's dinner!

Kay, Dad's carer, certainly made our home swing in the afternoons. Dad's face would light up when she arrived. In fact she became an honorary member of our family! In the afternoon they would watch cricket on TV or the *Afternoon Show* or a sentimental film and sometimes she would do some ironing for me. So while she was in the kitchen ironing, Dad would be saying his Rosary in the breakfast room. They would have a race! She would say "I bet ye I'll be finished the ironing before you finish your Rosary!"

On Saturdays, I had a couple of hours to myself. Kay would stay with Dad while I went into town to an exercise class. Then I would have a massage which would last one whole hour –bliss! A light lunch in the Carriage Restaurant, Wicklow St. –long since gone and sadly missed– was a real treat. Meeting up with someone whom I hadn't met for ages, was always a joy. I reckon that because of this weekly treat, I was able to keep going.

Each evening after a simple tea, like scrambled eggs on toast, the evening ritual would commence. *Coronation Street* first on TV and then whatever documentary was on that night.

Before all that, we would have our daily constitutional up and down the hall. Dad's legs had let him down by now and his neck was constantly encased in a hard collar. I would have to hold onto him tightly as we walked up and down, up and down. His request was that I put on the recording of Verdi's 'Rigoletto' which he adored. The soloists were his favourites, Pavarotti, Sutherland and Milnes. What a combination of fabulous voices. I had to sing the soprano line and he would attempt the tenor line, which was now impossible for him. What were we like?! But we would laugh and enjoy every moment. Dad had a lovely tenor voice and I have fond memories of him singing at family gatherings.

Rigoletto is mainly about the relationship between a father and daughter. The two duets in the opera which reflected our relationship were 'Figlia! Mio Padre' and 'Parla… siam soli'. In both of these, Rigoletto is warning his daughter Gilda about the dangers that surround her in life.

Dad insisted on sleeping upstairs and I was close by in my own room with the door wide open so I could get to him quickly if he had breathing problems. He would take ages to climb the stairs, but every night when we arrived in his bedroom, he would write on his slate "we made it once more".

Almost two years into the disease, most muscles in his body had ceased to function and as we had been told he probably would choke in the end. And so he did. He recovered slightly and by the time I had dashed home from the office, he was ready for his last journey into hospital. I was so glad that Kay had been with him. She was wonderful. He waved goodbye to his beloved home and got into the rear of the car with one of my brothers while I drove. The journey was horrendous as it was late afternoon and traffic was building as people made their homeward bound journeys, which we were ironically also doing; Dad was going to his real home in the next world. I flagged down a Garda on a motorbike and he drove out in front of us and got us to the hospital quickly. We settled Dad into bed there and he rested for a few hours and actually had a little sleep. Three days later, on 1st November 1985, he died peacefully, almost two years to the day since we got the diagnosis.

When I eventually returned home, the house felt so empty. I went up to my bedroom and put on the CD of the highlights of 'Rigoletto' and I sang it through loudly. It was a tremendous help to let all my emotions out as I had held them in check for the past two years. I was exhausted and very emotional when I opened my bedroom door to return to the family. One of my aunts, Dad's twin sister, was sitting outside on the top step of the stairs crying. She too was a singer. She told me that the music had helped her to come to grips with the great loss of her much loved brother. We both hugged each other and cried some more.

NUALA SMITH

SNOW BOOTS THAT FIT

New Year's Eve in Barbados. I'm at the Paradise Beach Club. It's 1970 and a steel band is playing to the warm velvet sky. I'm with a drummer from Montreal. He's tall and blonde and a laugh.

Normally I'd be delighted with him. But not tonight. Tonight is agony as I'm desperately in love with another man. Alex, the handsome dark-eyed Slav who's been staying in our guest house, up the coast.

But now Alex is gone. He left a week ago for work in Toronto and I've been inconsolable since.

Through a torrent of tears I saw him off at the airport.

"Come to Canada, Dolly?" he'd asked for the umpteenth time and the way he called me "Dolly" with a 'th' sound, was yet another thing I adored about him.

Here, my new date parks me with an umbrella-ed rum, jumps behind his drums, winks over, crashes the cymbals. But as the dancers samba past, I make up my mind.

Next morning, with my airline staff ticket, I glide past Barbados's sparkling seas to the airport once more. I make it to Toronto by nine that night.

Down the aircraft steps in my sandals, I'm oblivious to this minus five, as airport lights shine on snow. Minutes away, the adored one is waiting.

A man in a donkey coat and knitted hat waves both arms as I emerge. Though barely a week since I've seen him, he seems smaller. Throwing his arms round me, he smells of cigarettes. We laugh at my sandals, and set off in the car I've admired already in the photos.

His home is the top of Mrs Krezminska's house. As he opens the door, she appears at the end of the narrow hall, a cat clutched to her aproned chest, frowns at Alex, and vanishes. There's a smell of cabbage cooking.

Upstairs, his flat consists of a kitchen with a gas fire, a dark green bathroom and two box rooms, which he informs me, we must use for the moment as "Mrs Krezminska is Polish and very strict" but we'll be getting married soon and then "everything" will be all right. That first night, with snow falling outside, we snuggle by the gas fire, eating salami while Alex talks plans.

After he'd left for work on my first morning, I set out to buy snow boots. Banks of blackened snow line our street but the blue overhead is thrilling. I am striking out into my new world.

The boots I fall for say a lot, but I don't see that till much later. Yellow, fake seal fur, mid-calf, wooly lining —and half price; but they are a bit tight.

"They'll stretch" the girl says, "you'll break them in".

That evening, Alex stuffs them with damp newspaper when I display my blistered heels. Breaking in boots is part of life to him. He has lived in refugee camps on his journey from Yugoslavia, before Toronto.

I get work in a typing pool in an oil company. Most nights we sit, eating off a tray, watching the game shows he adores. His other delight is the 'agony aunt' section of the Toronto Mail. "Dear Abby" he reads them out to me, fascinated by these relationship dilemmas. The English is simple too. Privately I find them silly. But I smile along, as expected.

Fridays, we're at the church's Immigrants' Club, playing bingo with people from China, Portugal, you name it, and where I seem to be the only person who speaks English. Conversations are heavy going.

Secretly, I begin to long for Larry Murphy's pub and the craic in Baggot Street.

As the weeks pass, and he brings me deeper into his immigrants' world, I feel a growing fear that I have made a terrible mistake –and not only with my yellow boots, which by the way are still agony after several outings.

I don't remember my last night there. But I do remember our parting at the airport, in tears. As we hold each other for the last time.

I know, deep down, I'm leaving for good, and maybe he does too.

For a while on the flight, I continue to weep –for those brown eyes as I turned for gate 43; for that final "Come back soon Dolly?" for the pain I will cause with the letter I will soon send; for my now vanished dream.

In seat A17, I ease my feet from those cruel snow boots and dab my eyes as we roar down the runway. I am not to know of course that in less than a year I will hear that Alex has married an Air France hostess and is a regular on the beaches of Barbados.

BRIGID MURPHY

RADIO LUXEMBOURG

While going through a biscuit tin hidden away at the back of my wardrobe, in among old postcards and bits and pieces, I came across an old diary for the year 1961. It was a small red bound Young Folks Diary for Girl Guides and Boy Scouts. Inside the front cover was a picture of girl guides holding candles with a tag line "No electricity? We shall learn our knots by candlelight!"

On flicking through the pages virtually every date has an entry and on reading more closely I found entries that brought back memories of a period in my life that was both difficult and yet entertaining.

I was thirteen years old and a patient in Linden –a clinic for children with cardiac problems, situated near Stillorgan, Co. Dublin. I was in a large ward with nine other girls. Other wards had boys and also young children.

In one entry it said Rosaleen Ferris got her radio repaired. Great news as we loved listening to Radio Luxembourg when lights were out.

Radio Luxembourg –why don't you make a date with 208 your station of the stars– was very popular at the time. On Sunday night the top twenty hits was presented by Barry Alldis. Some of the popular tunes at the time were: *Stuck on you* –Elvis Presley; *Cathy's Clown* –The Everly Brothers; *Running Bear* –Johnny Preston; *Save the last dance for me* –The Drifters; *Livin Doll* –Cliff Richard.

Elvis Presley was very popular with a string of hits –*Stuck on you*; *Are you lonesome tonight*; *Surrender*; *Such a night*, to name a few. One of the girls in the ward, Mary Doyle, was mad into Elvis Presley. She was very vocal in her adoration of him. I loved Cliff Richard. Cliff was very good looking and had a number of hits around that time, *Please don't tease me*; *Livin Doll*; *Travelling light*; *The young ones*. The ward was fairly evenly divided between Elvis and Cliff fans and a few good rows were had as to which was more popular. Mary would hop out of bed and confront anybody who criticised Elvis. She had to be reminded to get back into bed or else...

The DJs on Radio Luxembourg were almost as famous as the pop stars. Names such as David Jacobs and Pete Murray spring to mind.

One of the girls decided to write to Radio Luxembourg and was delighted to receive a package with ten authographed photos of Pete Murray, one for each of us.

In another diary entry I succeeded in getting an authographed photo of Adam Faith. There was a competition among us to see who could get the most autographed photos of stars.

> *Sunday, 19th February.*
> *Bus strike is on. Mammy didn't come to see me. It is first time.*

> *Monday, 20th February.*
> *Mammy came to see me. She cycled out. Had chips for tea.*
> *They were gorgeous.*

The bus strike lasted for a number of weeks and it meant some children didn't have visitors as their parents depended on the bus to travel. My intrepid mother cycled the long journey out as that was the only Sunday she missed visiting me.

I spent a fascinating time reading through the diary and remembering some of the girls who were patients there. We had become close and were concerned for each other, especially if one had to go to the hospital for tests or a procedure.

It has been many years since I was in the clinic, but it has left me with an abiding appreciation of the ability to get out of bed and live my life, while also giving me a fond remembrance of Radio Luxembourg –your station of the Stars!

NUALA SMITH

UMBRELLAS

Umbrella. Parapluie. Don't you love those words? —how they roll off the tongue. Picture the *Umbrellas of Cherbourg*.

I'm walking towards my meeting today, sporting the red umbrella I bought in Singapore. It's not actually raining yet, but I put it up anyway as I love its colours over my head.

From the Chinese market in Singapore, for about three euros, I chose it for its scarlet background. But the Chinese umbrella-makers didn't stop there. Oh no. On its bright red, they scattered gold leaves with purple and green centers. They made tiny blue dragons poke their heads out between those leaves.

So I'm here on a damp Bray morning, roofed under a canopy of carefree, singing brilliance. I fancy my grey coat picks up the glow from above.

Secretly, I've always yearned for a fabulous umbrella. But thrifty creature that I am, I've baulked at their crazy prices, reminding myself that no one's going to see it in the rain.

In fancy shops, I've fingered those fabulous creations with their scalloped edges, their long bone handles and their sophisticated hues.

I've even coveted the kiddies' ones of see-through plastic with black ears on top, or those ladybird spots with red trimmings. But somehow, I always resorted to the bottom of the range, black, foldup at 3.99 in Dunnes.

Then my stylish friend Marie, who has a beautiful straight nose and impeccable taste, lost her reason –in my mind– and paid over a hundred euros for the most divine creation of an umbrella, on a trip to France.

This, confirming her undoubted refinement, is of coffee and cream lace, its generous dome topped off by a serious gold spike. Skirting its rim are cream lace ruffles that immediately catapult you to Audrey Hepburn and her *Fair Lady* triumph at Ascot. And who doesn't want to look like Eliza?

On a showery spring day last year my stylish friend was invited to a fancy lunch at Aras An Uachtaran. There she is now in the souvenir photo, smiling triumphantly from under those perfect frills.

So maybe that's what pushed me over the edge? For on my way home from Australia through Singapore this year, I found the Chinese market.

Sweltering in thirty five degrees, I shimmied up and down its stalls, mesmerised by their wares. Silk dressingowns in wild colours, pinks, purples, royal blues, scattered with gold fire eaters, pashminas in cottons, silks, lace and net: acres of beautiful cushions, tonnes of non-essentials, for half nothing.

And then I got to umbrellas. There they were, fabulous shades, in all sorts of shapes and sizes, small, medium, large, flat, and conical. Not a whiff of a black one. Dizzying choice, and for me, at last, abandon.

Finally, like a debutante surrounded by suitors, I reluctantly chose one. My perfect scarlet and yellow. Dainty, fold up and bright, loud, bordering on brash. Insistent, optimistic, cheery, unaware and uninterested in my home town's dark winter days.

So now, on the seafront in Bray, I hurry along in the rain, my feet encased in my heaviest boots, but over my head, my shelter of delight. And when I feel the tug of the wind, I'm fully prepared to be a Gene Kelly, or a Mary Poppins, for didn't you always want to dance like that too?

KIERAN DUNNE

THE STREAM OF LIFE

Some time ago I listened to a recorded interview with the late John B. Keane where he expressed his great love of walking by the river —no doubt his local Listowel River Feale. This is not an unusual pastime. In the latter half of the eighteenth century, Brian Merriman commenced his famous poem, The Midnight Court, with the lines which I have translated from the Irish:

"It is usual for me to walk by the bank of the river
The fresh grass and the heavy dew"

I lived in the lovely valley of the Munster Blackwater, a beautiful river, but still notable for its threatening floods. On hearing John B. Keane, I thought of a little stream, a tributary to that famous river which I loved in my youth. I reflected on how close the various moods and transformations of that stream resembled life's journey.

There was a boy
Who spoke to streams
Little streams
Just chattered back

Rains came
Streams changed to floods
A boy stands now, forlorn
Waiting for a stream reborn

Standing on the soggy bank
The boy withdraws.
Water, oft friend, now foe
In violence penetrates the earth
Above, below

Yesterday the stream was pure
Rounded pebbles and polished stones
Mosaic-like quilted
Its peaceful bed.

Today, blobbing debris
Ragged-clad bushes
Fringe its frothy pools
While fragile banks disperse their muddy load
The streams once pure floor, obscured.

A new dawn breaks,
Stillness scorns the receding flood
The boy, now a man, beholds
A stream being reborn

Such is life, its dark floods
Ever rising and abating,
Until a final calmness
A new and blessed world
So signalled by a stream of sacred water
Is awaiting.

THE CONTRIBUTORS

THE EDITOR

Cathy Fowley has a deep interest in life stories from an academic, human and personal perspective. This interest arose from a long-term passion for literature and particularly memoirs, which formed part of her doctoral research on blogging, and which informs her work with the Intergenerational Learning Programme in Dublin City University, where she designs and teaches life-writing modules for older people. She passionately believes that ordinary people have fascinating stories, and that age gives more meaning to those stories. She has yet to find someone whose story didn't teach her something new.

THE AUTHORS

Kieran Dunne, B.A. Hons, Dublin, Mallow, Co. Cork, retired Civil Servant, keen interest in Irish History and Literature, special interest in G.A.A., particularly the fortunes of the Cork Hurlers and Footballers.

Vera Hickey was born and reared in Co. Wicklow. She is wife of Michael and mother of three daughters and two grandchildren.

Thanks to DCU Intergenerational Learning Programme, this is her first attempt at writing.

Arlene McAllister was educated by the Dominicans from an early age. After her Leaving Certificate, she went to Secretarial College and was then employed in the family business, where she spent 33 happy and very busy years and became a Director/Secretary of the Company. Arlene took early retirement in order to pursue other interests. Her passion from a young age, was classical music. She presented a lunch time classical music programme for the Mater Hospital Radio, and a Sunday Serenade programme on NEAR FM. She was then invited to give extra-mural Music Appreciation Courses in two schools, which she did for seven happy years. She is still a singing member of The Culwick Choral Society. In retirement she studied languages, yoga, mindfulness, and meditation, and still attends Fitness League classes regularly. Most of all she loves to walk her dog Amber in the fresh air!

Michael Morris was born in London, 1944. He was brought up from the age of two in Dublin's Northside, first in Dominick Street and then in Finglas. At 15 he was apprenticed as a compositor to a small commercial printers and at 23 went to work with the Irish Press for 27 years until it collapsed. At that stage he had moved into journalism and with the closure of the firm went freelance and worked for The Irish Times, Evening News, Sunday Tribune, and the RTE Guide. Michael then worked in RTE as Chief Sub Editor for almost 15 years.

Brigid Murphy is married with two grown up children. She retired a few years ago after a long working life and is busy discovering all that is available for older people. She has rediscovered reading and is also working hard at moving outside her comfort zone.

Michael O'Sullivan is one of the men from God knows where, namely, the village of Dromahane, Mallow, Co. Cork. He arrived there directly from a nursing home in Cork city, where he was born in 1931. There he remained until he completed his secondary school education at the Patrician Academy, Mallow in 1949. He entered the Irish Civil Service in February 1949, serving in four departments, Posts and Telegraphs, Social Welfare, Industry and Commerce and Defence, but the vast bulk of his working life was in Defence. His roles in that department frequently included acting as ministerial speechwriter. He graduated in Commerce at Trinity College, Dublin in 1957 and for many years was a member of the Eblana Toastmasters Club, the second such club to be formed in Ireland. He was a founding member and first president of that club. On retiring from the Department of Defence in 1988, he lectured at the Dublin Institute of Technology for 5 years and, most recently, has pursued some courses at Dublin City University. He and his wife Myra, who celebrated their 50th wedding anniversary, now live in Donabate Co. Dublin. They have three daughters, one living in Connemara and two in the USA.

Kay Philpott was born in Dublin, and educated by the Presentation nuns. She worked in the Civil Service until her marriage and returned there when she was widowed, until retirement. Kay has ten children (all currently living in Ireland) and 16 grandchildren. Her favourite hobbies are writing and crosswords.

Dan Redmond, ex ground operations, Aer Lingus. "Egged on by our tutor, I discovered my past".

Nuala Smith was born in Drogheda in 1946, she has one sister and one brother. She grew up in Glasnevin, worked in AIB, Aer Lingus, UCD, ran a vegetarian restaurant 'Food for Thought' in Dun Laoire for 2 years, then moved to San Francisco, where she ran a small herbs'n'spices business. She came back to Dublin in the 1980's, opened garden centre in Bray - where she still lives. Nuala has one daughter. She has written for Sunday Miscellany, and published short stories and articles in various newspapers and magazines. She is currently working on her memoir after participating in Life Writing classes in DCU.